First, the Reflection

Poems by Diane Wahto

Spartan Press
Kansas City, MO
spartanpresskc.com

Copyright © Diane Wahto, 2019
First Edition 1 3 5 7 9 10 8 6 4 2
ISBN: 978-1-950380-48-0
LCCN: 2019944814

Design, edits and layout: Jason Ryberg
Cover image: Sandra Loux
Author photo: Rae Cuda
All rights reserved. No part of this publication may be reproduced or transmitted in any form or by any means, electronic or mechanical, including photocopying, recording or by info retrieval system, without prior written permission from the author.

The author would like to thank the editors of the following publications where some of these poems first appeared:

"The Discovery of the Bahamas," *Mikrokosmos,* Volume 33, Spring 1987.
"Stage Directions," *Mikrokosmos*, Volume 33, Spring 1987
"First, the Reflection," *365 Days Poets,* Volume 2016.
"Corner Shrine," *The 365 Days Poets,* Volume 2. 2018.

TABLE OF CONTENTS

Early Morning Jazz / 1

Betts on Piano / 2

The Rental House on Normal Street / 3

Dancing at Stage One / 4

Dark Dancing / 5

Improvisation / 6

Kitchen Dance / 7

First the Reflection / 8

Line in the Sand / 10

Military Discount / 12

News / 13

Seeking Refuge / 14

Shadow / 15

Raven Rock / 16

Somebody Is Always Watching / 17

Detective Novel / 19

Corner Shrine / 20

The Discovery of the Bahamas / 21

Missing Person / 24

Crime / 25

Hitchhikers / 26

Crossing the Desert in the Summer of Love / 27

Mazatlán / 28

Mountain / 29

One Degree Above the Equator / 30

Rain in the Tropic of Capricorn / 31

Vacation / 32

Driving Away from the Sun / 33

At the Edge / 34

Flying to Canada / 35

Not Done / 36

My Mother Calls Me / 37

Wonder Bread / 38

Upon Reading The Second Sex While
   Visiting My Mother / 39

The Truck Driver Updates His Log Book / 40

Escape / 42

Mirror / 43

Letters from my Mother / 44

The Magic of Inanimate Objects of the House / 45

The Weight of Sunday Morning / 46

When We Were Strangers / 47

First Sight / 48

In the Café / 49

Matinee at Café Bel Ami / 50

Lemon Gelato / 51

Stage Directions / 52

Stasis / 53

One of Those Nights   /   55

Fantasy   /   56

Well Done   /   57

Dark Matter/Dark Energy   /   58

Anomie   /   59

I Am Ocean   /   60

I Will Write Truth   /   61

Jupiter in Opposition   /   62

Pat Math   /   63

Monday Morning, Early Spring   /   64

To Patrick who loves my poetry, is amazed by it, often sends it to friends.

Early Morning Jazz

As the sun comes up,
Tony sits in his truck,
door wide open to air
of a chilly November
morning. His jazz goes
around the neighborhood.
A fully satisfying sound.
Improvisation on a theme
that plays itself out in
back and forth notes
among musicians who know
magical music in their souls,
music that touches the essence
of all who listen, all who dance
to a tasty rhythm, slightly tart,
an ear feast right at sunup.

Betts on Piano

Betts knew color through his nicotine-
stained fingers stroking across black
and white keys, through notes rising
from steel buried deep in the belly
of the brown beast. Nights, he tapped
his white cane or held a friend's arm
to walk to the basement club where hipsters
riffed their lives in the language of instruments,
where men and women danced to shake
away what broke their hearts day after day.
Betts' pale, pock-marked face crinkled
in smile, his head thrown back, recalled,
his last sight of color, the red of his mother's
rose bush as it faded slowly into black.
He was four. After, he did not see color,
only heard it in the music that filled dark hours.

The Rental House on Normal Street

He centers Mingus's "Ah Um" on the record player,
places the needle down on one track. "Fables of Faubus"
time after time. He pours Jack Daniels into a water glass,
later grabs the bottle neck in his stubby-fingered fist,
chugs, walks the floor, keeps pace with the walking bass.
Nights, Bob, the blind piano player, comes by,
sits on the ragged couch, chain smokes,
flicking his ash just wide of the old distributor cap
he holds in one skinny hand, cigarette hanging over the lip.
High in the invisible air, fingers of his other hand
make out a tune on the piano in his head. The man spends
days alone, thinks about the wife, the baby, gone.
Does not miss them. The landlady crosses the expanse of grass
between her big house and the small one in back,
asks him if he tortures piglets, the only way she knows
to describe the agony of sound that floats
through her summer windows in the night.
His life a wreck, his car a wreck. Some woman
will sit next to him at the bar, find him irresistible,
bed him, later call a friend and through sobs,
hiccup tales of his betrayal.

Dark Dancing

At the middle school dance, the seventh
grader says she can hardly wait for eighth
grade, can hardly wait to be old enough
to dance on the other side of the gym
where the lights are dim, where girls
and boys dance close. Dark dancing,
she calls it, even though she says she's
nervous about dancing close, something
she hasn't yet learned to do. I could tell
her a few things about dark dancing,
about a long-legged man who loved
to dance under low lights, who knew old
steps, made up new ones on a whim.
Then the lights came up, the music
slowed, then stopped, the long-legged
man learned a new dance to new music,
under different lights, these quite bright.

Dancing at Stage One

The last night of the festival,
dancers crowd in the dust
in front of Stage One. The long-
legged man says, *Let's dance.*
New Grass Revival launches
into "Don't Stop Now."
Two guitars, banjo, mandolin,
John Cowan's voice rising into
the clear September night.
We whirl, touch, separate,
touch, separate,
my skirt circling one way,
then another. We laugh,
fall into each other.
I watch the long-legged man disappear
into the dark, into the enveloping gloom.

Improvisation

She met a man who loved motorcycles,
morel mushrooms, Mingus. Her monody
developed off-beat harmonies, atonal
jazz riffs. Her dance became a whirl
of color, steps her feet had never
tried before. She created new trails
through unexplored woods, swam
in cold waters off sun-warmed
beaches. A drumbeat, the rhythm
of her life, the tempo altered
when she least expected.

Kitchen Dance

We whirl, turn, reel from cabinet
to refrigerator, to pantry, to drawer,
as roast chicken aroma fills the kitchen.
We are careful not to step on toes,
trip on feet, moving quickly around
the space, not small, but our movements
make the room seem crowded
as we try to cook a meal together.
Yes, they say, too many cooks
spoil the broth, but somehow
we beat the odds as we sit
at the table to savor our food.

First, the Reflection

The Vietnamese neighbor comes to the door
with his offering of steaming, aromatic egg rolls.
In English still broken after all these years,
he says, We are celebrating a grandchild's
birthday and we want to share. His smile
unbroken except for the wrinkles that form
a shell on his brown face. We take the gift,
bows all around, thank him. At first bite,
we taste the flavor of the far off place,
the place that came alive on our TV screens,
in our dreams and nightmares so many years ago.

Years ago, I walked on the Mall, came
upon the Wall. Stunned to tears, my image
caught in the gabbro slab mingling with the names
of those lost to a theory based on a parlor trick
played with wooden tiles used in a game played
by old men in small town dark bar afternoons.
Soon, my focus takes in names, sons, brothers,
fathers, friends. My brother's name not there,
his safe homecoming freeing us to breathe again.

Yesterday, we found the body of the baby squirrel
our little dog had attacked the day before. Rescued
from the dog's grip, the tiny animal limped away

too injured to withstand the assault, the shock
of sudden violence. Predator, prey. Animal power
unchecked by reason or love. We threw the tiny body
into the trash barrel so the dog would not violate
it further. The names on the Wall beyond violation.
Only their dim reflection remains.

Line in the Sand

Ever shifting.
The old paradigms are straw
blown by the slightest wind.
Boundaries waver, grow dim.
Collective memory caught
in a net leaves only the myths
of a decayed culture.
The young, the strong,
the fresh-faced march
in lockstep to strange
lands are they cry,
Freedom.

Pride-filled gray sages
see them off with a cheer
Lost in the haze of battlefield
smoke, the young see enemy
in innocence. Transfixed
by shiny medals by tales
of courage, by the smell
of blood, the folks back home
parrot, *Freedom.*

Military Discount

It is Memorial Day. He has put the flag
out. We talk about war, its futile nature,
his father who stormed the beach on D-Day,
my father whose high blood pressure, flat
feet kept him out. My four uncles who
returned unscathed, one to die of alcohol,
one the victim of a senseless murder.
Cancer, obesity, and arrogance got another.
My grandmother with her small flag fringed
in gold, the bullet she kept on the buffet,
the acrid, metallic, smell living
in my memory from childhood.

Today, he, who was drafted as a CO, walks
to the memorial service by the river. He will
mingle with other vets, those who have no
idea that he hates all war. He feels a kinship
with these men, some of whom he might
have tried to heal, to ease their pain when
their torn bodies were flown to safe haven.
Scarred with battle wounds, they walk
with their haunted eyes hooded from the sun.

Tomorrow, he will think about kitchen
renovations, pull out his military ID card
with the number that says he is indeed a veteran.
Choosing to shop at hardware stores, carpet
centers, wherever else he can find to get
a military discount, he brings bounty
back with figures to show how much
he saved. Useless as a soldier, he refused
to carry a gun, to take promotions. Adept
at treating the wounded, restoring life,
and limbs, whenever possible, he served
a purpose. Then he came home, took
off the uniform, walked on the grass
of his grandmother's lawn, said, *Yes,
I'm free. I'm free.*

News

Garrison in five, he yells to me in the kitchen.
I wash the morning dishes, sit in the living room
to hear the poem. First, five minutes of state news.
I hear that our elected officials have concerns—
pornography, its effects on those who view it.
Something I never give a thought to. Our elected
officials also want to dictate font and size, women
being unable to make out any print other than
Times Roman, 12 point, when they make
the tough decision some women make.
Our state is in decline, but that is set aside
for our elected officials must use their hours
in the pursuit of what is good and pure, protect
those of us who lack the wit to protect ourselves.
Finally, Garrison comes on, his Minnesota voice
in a banter that takes us to a better place, a place
a safe place, a place that needs no protection.

Seeking Refuge

Where do you find hope or solace
under a cold sky that is not your sky,
far away from the land that means loss
to a land where the earth provides
only hard ground to ease your nights,
where no roof deflects winter winds,
no warm kitchen aromas brighten
the end of a day spent in mundane
pursuits. This lonely refuge will
keep you safe for now, your child
holding a teddy bear, kept warm
in a puffy jacket, free from alarm
for now, roams the unfamiliar
landscape, explores a new world
before he barely knows the old
you have left so far behind.

Shadow

What is left is the shadow of a man
against the only wall left standing,
the wall pink, the shadow a gray
outline, outstretched arms raised
like a mouth open in a scream
of surprise. This man a reluctant
actor in a play with no rehearsal,
a drama with no denouement, all
substance shattered into bits spread
like poison through the indifferent
sky. This man a puppet controlled
by an unseen hand in the shadow
show that still hangs hidden
above our heads, lies below
the ground. Shadow people
wait for the word, the end
of the agony of suspense.

Raven Rock

A place for the government to hide
while the rest of us, unprotected, die.
A vision of men in suits, ties, shoes
shined by the man who set up shop
near the Capital cafeteria. He was not
invited to the party in the bunker.
Well-dressed women, jackets, pencil
skirts showing well-honed bodies.
Lucky children whose parents found time
to bring them from home to safety.
The others, well, they can bend under
their school desks as the mushroom
cloud fills the innocent sky.

And what of the steaks coming from cows,
once peacefully grazing on high pastures,
now turned into phantom animals?
Do our leaders plan to install freezers
huge enough to keep food for everyone?
Or will food fights break out among
the well-suited hidden underground?

And when will those brave leaders emerge?
And what will they find left to love?
For some, the slow ruination of the earth
has become a second's piece of work.
Their goal has been met. Yet, oil will
be hard to come by in the ruination.

Somebody Is Always Watching

I see the photo of you naked
kneeling beside your fresh-dug grave.
You look so soft.

There was that night in Paris
before the war.
We danced then talked until morning
at the café. You wore your black dress.

They say you spat on your killer,
 soiling the uniform of the young lieutenant.
The records show he died at the Russian front,
 his body frozen under snow until spring.

Smoke curls from the cottage chimneys in the village
near the woods.
At the moment the first bullet hits your breast,
the cobbler taps the last nail
into the sole of the priest's black shoe.
A child throws a ball against the well
ignoring his mother's call for supper.
A man and woman meet under the bridge
shivering in their thin coats. I hide
in the cellar of Vera's house
among the turnips and leeks
put by for the winter. I wait for word from George.

Safe passage across the lines.
I tried to warn you.

I put my hands over my ears
to shut out the faint explosions.

Detective Novel

The foreshadowing sets the reader up
for a satisfactory conclusion.
But who can tell what twists a plot
will take, or how many stumbling
blocks a protagonist can handle
before finally saying I'm tired
of living this fiction, of carrying
this impossible load? I cannot swim
these icy waters one more time.
I'm no longer lithe enough
to dodge bullets, don't have the moves
to evade the silver knives
flashing at my exposed abdomen.
No one with an ounce of pity
would expect this of another human
being, expect him to outwit,
outshoot, outrun, survive
so many adversaries
in the course of an average day.
Get your cheap thrills some other way.
I'm going out for a donut
and a cup of coffee.

Corner Shrine

After six shots rang out
in the quiet, sunny afternoon,
after one man slumped over
the steering wheel, another
man still alive,
after the police sirens,
after the yellow crime tape
closed off the street we drive
to take Annie to the park,
after lights illuminated the scene,
after the neighbor leaned her head
on her husband's chest, sobbed,
after dark came,
after the sun came up,
the shrine appeared.

Tall, thin candles inside glass vases,
white and red plastic roses,
a red balloon tied around the stop sign.
Hour by hour, new tributes bloomed
until the corner groaned
with loss and grief.
All young men, the dead man
a father, all engaged in a war
far away from us,
now too close
to shrug it off.

The Discovery of the Bahama

I.
The Woman Entertains Her Guest

This soft, soft sound—
silk dress against an arm.
Love, fetch me something cool to drink.
The diver found the body early
this morning. He said there was no sign
of foul play. You know, my dear,
I've heard it's a pleasant way to go.
Like being born but gentler.
Those who almost make it once
try and try again until they get it done.
His shoes were on the bank, right near
where he floated, stretched out straight,
not in the curl that bodies usually make
when they take in that much water.
his bait and empty pole were on the bank.

II.

The Diver Performs His Civic Duty

You can't see a damn thing
on the bottom of that scum.
Everything has to be done by feel.
Who would go to that hole to fish anyway?
They called me at 3 a.m.—I'd stayed up 'til 2
thinking I'd have the morning to sleep in.
It was 5:30 when I touched his foot,
And eight by the time they finished the report.
I make the city guys look bad—
they'd been all night searching
blind in the mud.
I have an instinct about these things.
Once you spot the shoes, you can divine
where the sap has laid his body.
I do this for the good of the cause—
the one thing I do almost no one can.

III.
The Fisherman Explains Love

Your dress floats just out of reach,
barely moving among the seaweed.
I want to touch it.
Don't move away. Come close.
I'm just a harmless fisherman
prepared to tell my lies.
Put your arms around me.
Let me feel your skirt against my legs.
Hold me tight. This ooze
of warmth and sleep chills me
to the bone.
We will laugh at sapphire fish.
I will fill a sea purse
with my blue-green change.
The color of your silk dress
and your eyes sometimes at dusk.

Missing Person

They think it might have been the avalanche
that buried her, but no one knew for sure.
She wasn't missed for days.
It could have been the lava that swallowed
everything up, including her
when the volcano blew one fine morning.

All they knew is one day she was gone
and after a time they saw she hadn't returned.
They said there was no point in looking:
if the lava got her there would be nothing
left to find. If it was the snow, well,
the spring thaw would be time enough.

Crime

Love and hate live close,
inseparable as loss,
intermingled, unidentifiable.
A whiplash across the heart,
a revelation so stark
it turns to rust the love
that once was a wall
holding strong against
a wind that blows ill
in the night of hate.

Hitchhikers

He leads them into the house,
into our sanctuary, doors open
in summer to catch a breeze.
Two hippie women, young,
slim. I, too, young, slim
from mothering three kids.
My matron face looms over
them, sends out a message
of housekeeping, laundry,
cooking meals, feeding pets.
Night comes, sleeping bags
rolled out on the living room
floor. In my upstairs bed,
I do not sleep. I listen
for footsteps on the stairs,
listen to my husband's
breathing. Morning,
a little breakfast, an egg,
some toast, coffee. I make
cheese sandwiches for
the road, face curled lips,
rolled eyes, my kitchen
a trap for those who
have taken to the road.

Crossing the Desert in the Summer of Love

*If you come to San Francisco, wear flowers
in your hair,* we hear on every radio
station between Michigan and Mexico.
We drive the black station wagon, miles
of sand and mountain. I wear my pink
sleeveless dress in the desert heat. Only
whores wear pants in Mexico, you say.
And I believe you. We get to the Sierra
Madres, you are sick from eating fried
turtle steak. I, a Pepsi propped between
my thighs, drive. Clouds below us on
the narrow, sinuous road. I don't dare
look down, but keep my eyes straight
ahead, teeth clenched with hope that
we stay on the road when we are overtaken
by rickety trucks or buses filled with people
who stare, you in the back of the black
car. I drive alone, my dress pulled up.

Mazatlán

Women in black shawls
barter for the morning
catch at seaside
fish stalls.

We walk.

A small boy wants to sell
a stinking, swollen blowfish.

By noon we take to our white
room and close the shutters.
The light hits everything:

sea

        sand

                plaza.

Across the square
a dog barks once.

Mountain

Over the flatlands, the mountain rises.
Granite impediment to my longing eyes,
my desire to know what lies beyond green
valleys, pine forests. My body strains
to break the bonds of the implacable choke,
the slate-colored barricade, a cloak,
a straitjacket that grips me within
the confines of the next crest, a moraine
set here by ancient, mindless passage
of glacier driving dirt, rock through age-
old landscapes, or by the stab, the thrust
of the ascent of earth's angry core, lust
become manifest, hardened over years.
Silent monolith harbors our unvoiced fear,
gives back nothing to our voiced appeal
but an empty echo, an unmoving wall.

One Degree Above the Equator

You have been here before, a time lost
in the jumble of familiar objects.
The car window distorts your face, distorts
the space beyond the window.
You have crossed a line. You might
as well be eyeless, invisible, a night
animal snuffling the odor of the ancient
one you will become. No walls separate
you from the sandy landscape. Two burros
stand flank to flank, one facing east,
one facing west, heads low against noon
sun. Nothing moves, nothing disturbs
stasis one degree above the equator.

Rain in the Tropic of Capricorn

Crossing the Sierra Madres,
we hide from tropical murders
of certain ambivalent loves.
Windshield wipers slosh away
great heaps of old, used-up stars
scattering like diamonds on this dirt road.
We call down the shaft of an abandoned
mine, hoping the mouthless bodies
will answer and swallow up our fear.
The glass fogs over from our heavy breathing.
We are here without visa in the city of love.
Here where calves' heads are skinned
and carried in tubs through the market,
where crowds defy gravity and hang
by their toes from the sky. It's too easy
to say we're at peace, but the saguaro
spread their arms over us in blessing.
A small sign divides the good from the evil
but it's possible to cross over in one leap.
A child says good-bye over and over,
And a letter arrives, the one we've been
waiting for, the one we open for news
of what is one the other side of the mountain.

Vacation

We stand on the shore of the Gulf
this brothy Alabama night,
dare each other into water
we can't see
except for phosphorescent edges of waves.
In the domain of whales, shellfish, manatees,
we are intruders.

You take one step, two,
then more, up to your chest.
Sand seeps from under my toes,
pulls me in after you.
I dig in deeper at the edge.
Fear's not the handle
that grips me, keeps me fixed
in place. It is the knowing if I leave
the safe shore for the water,
I will find safe habitat.

Driving Away from the Sun

The sun has set in the Flint Hills eons before time
gave names to sun and flint and hills. Before I, a child,
knew the cycles of time had definition, had names,
happened, every day different, every day the same.
Before I waded in the salt of distant oceans
on all sides of the wide world, of the expanse
of earth where we have staked our claim. Before
my daily toil, before we shaped a common lore
passed on through generations, truth and lies
caught in the knot crafted as the strong ties
that bound us and still bind us into the crux
of leery watchers of big-handed clocks
on the walls of our lives, ticking minutes
away as we drive the crowded streets.
We turn away from the sun, turn to face
the dark hills that will cover us with peace.

At the Edge

On the observation deck, the Niagara's roar
drowns out voices, thought, all that is rational.
Fist tight around the rail, you know your position
is precarious, sense the ease of a weightless fall
into that mist. So much depends on an upright
stance—the husband who stands beside you,
children who are waiting at home, a cat
who must be fed every day. No free fall
for those who are tied to the flesh of those
who occupy the house still waiting, the key
still fitting into the lock of the solid front door.

Fleeing to Canada

We took the test,
passed it, barely.
Both still young enough
to cross the Blue Water Bridge
over the St. Claire River,
both working at jobs
we could do in cyberspace.
We had income.
Both in good health.
Both ready
to leave it all behind.
But the dogs.
Five of them,
the collie too old
for travel.
All unemployed.
All at home in the big back yard.
The fence that kept them safe
kept us from fleeing.

Not Done

> *You're not done with your mother yet.* Allen Ginsberg

Not done with any of them, ever.
We find them in our veins, our
skin, the eyes which show us
what we see, ears to hear. We
can never escape what closed
us in, kept us safe, then closed
over us as we wriggled out
of the cocoon into a new cocoon.
I hear my mother's voice, hear
her call me from the back screen
door, her apron covering her dress,
her black shoes with the wedge
heels keeping her rooted. One
day, she will hang her apron on
a hook, never to be unhooked
again, she will wear tennis shoes,
slacks, want a car with more pick-up.
She will take plane trips with my dad.
No matter how high she flies, I will
never be free of her. Once, she let
me go free, relieved to have her
own freedom that came with mine.
Even so, I could never escape her,
she could never escape me. We will
go on forever together in the faces,
eyes, voices, the blood of all those
who come after.

My Mother Calls Me

I run free in this small town.
To the river to explore small caverns,
to the little grocery store where I buy
candy for a nickel. To the drugstore
to have a cherry Coke with friends.
Why today in this dream does she call me in?
Maybe she sees a hobo who will ask for a sandwich,
or the gypsy woman who walks by every day.
Could my mother be lonely, friendless,
gone now from everything she's always known?
I walk up the steps to the screen door where she stands
wearing her flower print dress, shoes
tied tight to support her polio damaged legs.
I reach out to open it as it disappears in an abyss
I cannot cross.

Wonder Bread

White as snow, soft as a pillow,
two slices slathered with mayonnaise.
Mom puts bologna between the bread,
sometimes ham sliced thin by the butcher
if she's feeling rich that day. Potato chips
sit in the package on the middle of the table.
Just my brothers and me. No conversation,
just eating, an occasional spat—little brothers
are the worst. My mother rarely joins us,
does laundry or housework. We don't
give her a second thought. She's Mom.
She has secret powers. We drink ice cold
Coke to wash it all down. Somehow,
we all survive to a decent age.

Upon Reading *The Second Sex* while Visiting my Mother

Pregnant with my second child, I sprawl
on my barely blooming belly across
my mother's bed. I read. In the kitchen,
she clanks pans out of cabinets, carries
plates, silverware to the dining table.
My first child watches cartoons in the den.
His giggles penetrate my concentration.
Still, I read and whisper, *Yes, yes,*
to the pillow propping up my paperback.
My husband elsewhere, working toward
another degree to improve our prospects
for a better life, unaware that I see my
better life far away in a two-room garret
on the *Rive Gauche* where I write novels
full of angst and painterly imagery. Papers
carrying my handwriting fall like stars
across the floor of the garret. I barricade
myself to write a novel of the glimmer
of love, sensual, pure. Gone wrong before a year
is out, the main character roaming bridges
over the Seine in evening fog, in search
of the one who will once again fulfill her life.
Nightly, I will join the *literati*, drink absinthe.
My glittering laugh will carry across the café
in homage to drunken *mots* from the mouths
of those whose names I know
only from book jackets.

The Truck Driver Updates His Log Book

He sits at the kitchen table, head down,
as he bears down hard on the pencil, writes
mileage, city names, route numbers
in the tablet with the tissue thin pages,
carbon paper behind each yellow page
to duplicate what he's writing. After
every trip he does this, turns each sheet
into the dispatcher, files his own sheet
in a cigar box the bedroom he shares
with his wife. It's not hard work, just
tedious, keeping track trip after trip,
mile after mile. I sit across the table,
listen to him mutter the names of cities.
St. Louis, then Dallas, Amarillo, places
that hold me fascinated, enlarge the small
world of my hometown, places I dream
of going to. What is never in the log,
his buddies on the road, Bus, Worth,
Carl, Johnny, Ernie Faulkner, killed
by a falling pop machine, men who are
fathers to my school friends, men
who stop to eat at brightly lit truck
stops at midnight, where they discuss
whatever it is men discuss when they're
on the road away from family or anything

that keeps them tied to home. Sometimes,
my dad mentions a waitress, how she flirts
with all the guys, gets good tips, raises
her two young boys alone, her mother
staying overnight to help her out. Our
mother stays silent, never pries, goes
about the business of keeping the house,
taking care of kids, reading her books
when he's on the road.

Escape

The dream drifts away into wisps,
remnants of it troubling my clouded brain.
Unlike the night I dreamed
I had many rings on my fingers.
Rings of gold and diamonds.
I took them off and put them on
in different combinations, delighted
at the sparkle of my hands,
wondered at my good fortune
to have such gems. When I awoke,
my hands were unadorned except
for the gold band we bought
at the pawn shop down the street
and my mother's wedding ring
with the little diamond sitting atop
a golden circle, a ring older than I am.

Mirror

Through the camera lens, I see my grandmother,
holding my sturdy first-born son in her arms.
The round cheeks of his serious face
turned to her face that mirrors his.
Across generations, they contemplate each other.
Tiny white flowers cover her dark housedress
Her tight-curled, short white hair haloes her face.
She holds my child, her great-grandchild. He is
the only child of mine she will hold, the others
born too late. Who knows how she felt
about babies, herself the mother to eight,
plus the one who died in childbirth. Yet,
she kept her patience with all of us, kept
sugar cookies in the jar in the kitchen,
cookies she had cooked from scratch
using a recipe I've never been able
to duplicate. She lives in all those
who have come after, whose lives
have moved on, who have carried
her with us wherever we alight.

Letters from my Mother

In her neat cursive, she sends family news,
names of neighbors who have died or moved,
town gossip. Among the musty envelopes,
I find a letter I wrote to her but never mailed.
I open it, read, *I've met a boy. He has ideas.*
He doesn't believe in Jesus, he says.
Wise of me at age nineteen not to send
that letter. The news would have made
my mother puzzled, sad. That boy asked
me where I kept my soul. The black
hole in my heart grew big for I knew
then I had no soul. At the bottom of the pile
I find my mother's letter with the news
about my dad, his mortal illness.
She could have called.
It's best she didn't.

The Magic of Inanimate Objects of the House

It was the brown recliner my father sat in,
the blue recliner my mother sat in,
the coffee table between them, shot glasses
holding his whiskey, her gin over ice,
a small crystal bowl of candy, an ashtray
for Dad's cigar ashes. It was the dining table
where we shared meals, where we argued
about politics, shared gossip about people
we knew or thought we knew. Kitchen chairs
spoke volumes.

Now, all is ordinary.
The light fades.
Nothing means more than it is.

The Weight of Sunday Morning

Empty hours sit on my shoulder,
Poe's raven whispering *Nevermore,*
in my ear. Wisps of memories come, go,
leave me reaching for an unbroken thread—
so the many miles traveled. Too many houses.
too many towns, cities, too many friends
gone or left behind. Too much life,
yet not enough to satisfy. The light
comes through the ivy over the small
window, the raven takes flight,
a breeze brushes my face.

When We Were Strangers

I Wish We Were Strangers Again. Judy Collins

You, your face behind a book,
looked up as I walked in the room.
Silence overtook the chatter,
people faded to wraiths. That
moment lives in your face,
now older, in your eyes, still
wrinkling when you smile,
the lilt in the voice, a certain
excited, hurried breathlessness
over trifles, to you momentous.
When I first saw your face,
when I first heard your voice,
in that too small room, the rest
of my life opened as you closed
your book.

First Sight

Some say love at first sight
is a myth, that eyes locked
across a room indicates near-
sightedness. Some say we
put too much faith in fairy tales,
believe that a prince on a white horse
will come to our rescue, will give
us the kiss that will wake us
from the snooze of boredom.
I say I need to rouse myself,
find my own white horse, ride
to my own rescue, find my own
path through the forest.

In the Café

They sit in the back at the red-topped,
round table, heads down, hands folded
near cups of untouched coffee growing
cold. A young man just out of boyhood,
a woman. He whispers, *If only.* She
her voice quiet, echoes, *If only.* Then,
Do you have your ticket? In my pocket.
The bus will be here in twenty minutes.
It is then they sip coffee, ask the waitress
for a warm-up, sip again, silent, their eyes
down, looking everywhere, not at each other.
He looks at his watch, stands, throws his
jacket over his shoulder, picks up his bag,
says, *Bye.* She stands, a small figure
next to his tall, lanky one, reaches up
to hug him, steps back. She watches
him go out the door, looks around
at people who look away, do not
look at her, do not want to see her.
She sits alone at the red table.

Matinee at Café Bel Ami

I wait for my friend who still grieves
for her husband, gone since spring.
The restaurant echoes with the din
of women discussing their lives.
One announces to the well-dressed
diners at her table, and to the room
at large, *I told her I don't need the drama,*

As tortured Hamlet cried,
The play's the thing.
How do we arrange life
with no drama to impel us forward,
to stage our moves, our entrances,
our exits, as we cross the stage,
hit our marks, those black pieces
of tape put down by the silent state manager
to define our poses as we declaim
our unscripted dialogue.

My friend arrives,
trails drama in her wake. We order wine.
She voices the mystery play of her loss.

Lemon Gelato

Tart explosion on the tongue,
sweet melt into the throat.
You savor the first taste.
Anticipation builds
for the next.
A dip of the spoon.
Spoon to lips.
Pleasure ghosts
a hidden smile.

Stage Directions

First consider the light.
The light must indicate
heavy summer air.
Air of storms.
Electric.

And the chairs on this bare stage.
Some wooden, some soft and worn.
Chairs for men and women who want
to sit in idiosyncratic forms
of abashment. Men and women
say the lines perfectly
each opening night.

Paint onto the backdrop these implements of daily life.
Garbage can, large, zinc.
Bathtub, white.
Indoor/outdoor carpet, green.
In the back yard, a line to hang the sheets.

Attention must be given to moment,
all action slow and unforgiving,
every tic faithfully duplicated.
All characters will end up at the same mark,
the mark where they started.

Stasis

Time holds, sound fades.
A man, a woman. Their lips
a pantomime of sound.
Their bodies a frieze.
Myself frozen by their
stance on the bridge
above me. Whispers
float into the arching
sky, fall to the rushing
river between us. Yet,
we are entwined, three
fates sealed as one,
caught in this intimacy
of intrusion. I will
my leaden legs
to walk along
the curved path.
One more glimpse
of her face, now
a lovely mystery. His
face, a mask, gives
nothing away. I seek
the solace of noise,
of movement,
companionship
of strangers untouched

by quietude. I don
my armor of daily
tasks, don't look
back.

They will always be there
in my waking hours,
my fretful nights.

One of Those Nights

Red silk rose
atop a slender stem
of green ribbon
wrapped around a wire.
The woman
with auburn hair
stands tall
in her gray winter coat,
brilliant in the air
that dances around her.
The woman of your dreams,
luminescent as ice.
The unattainable one,
she walks away
without a backward glance.
Forever young,
she leaves you
to empty fantasies.

She calls late one night.
You leave her to the answering machine.

Fantasy

You're in love with a fantasy, says Inez.
I'm in love with you, says Gil.
        From "Midnight in Paris"

Let us create a reality of diaphanous veils
through which the slightest breeze reveals
only a glimpse of gray sky beyond the fragile
threads, hiding what lies outside illusion, guile.
Yet, buried deep within that dim outer light,
the raw orb that may contain the one bright
star you have sought, the one piece to craft
anew a vision, unforeseen, yet wholly wrought.

Well Done

A Monty Python blue sky covered
with puffed-up white clouds spreads
over rain-greened landscape. Soon,
as I reach the crest of a hill, a fist
will appear, the long index finger
extended toward the small figures
below. Soon a booming voice will
sound a joyous cry. *Well done,*
will echo over the hills filled
with cattle, horses, wild flowers,
the wide highway that leads
to towns and cities, families
we love, places to visit. *Well
done. For once, you got it right.
Carry on, my children.*

Dark Matter / Dark Energy

Earthbound, we fail to see the invisible
force that pulls us downward, fail
to note our infinitesimal place in a large
universe, larger than our imagination.
What we are—fleas on the back
of the cosmic dog too huge
to comprehend—refutes
our single-minded egocentrism.

Anomie

Night stretches into a long train whistle.
Sleepless, you stare into the dark, think
about the stranger you will be when sun
illuminates the kitchen window shade.
The constant irritation of existence niggles
at you, so small you cannot see to swat
it as you stand solid for your own name.
Do you wait for one who might not come
or take your knapsack full of hope, push
off from shore and sail alone, satisfied
that you take only what you know, what
you can't bear to leave behind?

I Am Ocean

Inside me lives the sea salt water
that once covered this land, water
that sustains us, connects us to what
is around us, keeps us steady
as we walk through a world
often untethered to anything
we can hang onto. I look
inward, find my balance,
hope for the peace that comes
with connection, with the blue
of water, the green of land,
the white of the sands
as I wade into the ocean.

I Will Write Truth

When the rainstorm hits the house,
the roof leaks.

Wild animals
leave paw prints
on the kitchen floor.

Bronze men in suits
write urgent notes
on gilt-edged memo pads.

Forests shudder
when night heaves in upon them.

Buffalo play
by the side of the road.

Jupiter in Opposition

I was warned to watch out for it,
Jupiter in opposition to the sun.
It was to occur just as the sun set.
We could watch it from our west
windows, though I missed the epic
battle, I fear. My husband wanted his
supper. What was I to do? A man
has to eat. So I let Jupiter and the sun
fight it out as I cooked chicken
and noodles and a vegetable—
he is a meat and vegetable man—
and I missed the whole thing.
The sun rose again this morning
as usual, so I guess it didn't
sustain too many battle scars.
The status of Jupiter? Still
hanging in there, I suppose.

Pat Math

Home from Ace Hardware, he balances plastic bags
on the back of the couch, pulls out one by one
purchases for the house. Strong bug spray to kill
the midnight roaches that take over this old house
despite our best efforts, caulking material, two kinds,
to fix our bathroom walls. Super Glue, roach powder.
With each item, he tells me how much he saved,
including his military discount, how much we saved
by not going to Iowa this year, a savings
that paid for all these items. I call it Pat Math—
if we spend this on this we will save this.
If we don't do this, we have money to do that.
I balance the checkbook with bank math,
something he never sees. If he only knew
what I spend on lunches with friends,
favorite projects, saving public broadcasting,
saving the world with my small donations,
he would have to refigure his Pat math.
I let him exist in happy ignorance.
After all, he will keep this old house
in good repair. No complaints.

Monday Morning, Early Spring

Near the pond the horses stand.
The spotted mare with her brown foal.
The brown mares, bellies big.
They barely move and when they move
they touch, nose to quivering
flank. Cold spring mornings
when ice rims the pond, their breath
is rime. A road runs beside
the field, over a bridge, twists away.
The road never breaks
their ease of flesh, the gracious
distance of that field, that pond.

When my three sons left for college, I entered the MFA program at Wichita State University. I entered the buzz saw of critique workshops full of hope. However, after a few weeks I planned to drop out of the program, Robert Dana, a visiting professor from Iowa, said I should stay in the program. I eventually learned how to write poetry. Professor Bruce Cutler became my thesis advisor. He entered of my poems to the American Academy of Poet competition. I was awarded first place, with a check to go along with it. After I graduated with the MFA, I taught English Composition at Butler Community College, where I taught for forty plus years. I'm still writing poetry and getting published. I'm also a co-editor for three editions of 365, the anthology of poets who post to the Facebook, "365 Poems in 365 Days." I've published two books of poetry. Leap of Faith, is a self-published book with the help of my son and his MAC computer. My second book, *The Sad Joy of Leaving*, was published by Blue Cedar Press. As president of District 5 of the Kansas Authors Club, I've gotten to know poets from around the state. I also belong to four poetry groups, Poets in Hiding, Women Who Write, Thursday Group, and Basement Bards. I owe thanks to everyone in those groups for their close and careful reading of my work. I especially appreciate Roy Beckemeyer, Robert Dean, and Ronda Miller for their support. In May, my poem, "In Answer to W.B Yeats," I received the first place award in the Kansas Voices for the traditional poetry category, as well as winning the best poet award. My husband, our little dog Annie, and I live in Wichita's Old Town in a house that's almost a hundred years old.

This project was made possible, in part, by generous support from the Osage Arts Community.

Osage Arts Community provides temporary time, space and support for the creation of new artistic works in a retreat format, serving creative people of all kinds — visual artists, composers, poets, fiction and nonfiction writers. Located on a 152-acre farm in an isolated rural mountainside setting in Central Missouri and bordered by ¾ of a mile of the Gasconade River, OAC provides residencies to those working alone, as well as welcoming collaborative teams, offering living space and workspace in a country environment to emerging and mid-career artists. For more information, visit us at www.osageac.org

www.ingramcontent.com/pod-product-compliance
Lightning Source LLC
Chambersburg PA
CBHW030131100526
44591CB00009B/597